MAURICE SENDAK
King of the Wild Things

by Jodie Shepherd

Content Consultant

Nanci R. Vargus, Ed.D.
Professor Emeritus, University of Indianapolis

Reading Consultant

Jeanne M. Clidas, Ph.D.
Reading Specialist

Children's Press®

An Imprint of Scholastic Inc.

Library of Congress Cataloging-in-Publication Data
Names: Shepherd, Jodie, author.
Title: Maurice Sendak: king of the wild things/by Jodie Shepherd.
Description: New York : Children's Press, an imprint of Scholastic, Inc.,
[2017] | Series: Rookie biographies | Includes index.
Identifiers: LCCN 2016030328| ISBN 9780531222911 (library binding) | ISBN
9780531227725 (pbk.)
Subjects: LCSH: Sendak, Maurice—Juvenile literature. | Authors,
American—20th century—Biography—Juvenile literature. |
Illustrators—United States—Biography—Juvenile literature. | Children's
stories—Authorship—Juvenile literature.
Classification: LCC PS3569.E6 Z83 2017 | DDC 741.6/42092 [B] —dc23
LC record available at https://lccn.loc.gov/2016030328

Produced by Spooky Cheetah Press
Design by Judith Christ-Lafond

Printed in China 62

SCHOLASTIC, CHILDREN'S PRESS, ROOKIE BIOGRAPHIES™, and associated logos are trademarks
and/or registered trademarks of Scholastic Inc.

1 2 3 4 5 6 7 8 9 10 R 26 25 24 23 22 21 20 19 18 17

Photographs ©: cover main: UPP/TopFoto/The Image Works; cover background, back cover
background: Leyasw/Shutterstock, Inc.; 3: BillionPhotos.com/Fotolia; 4: Patrick Downs/Getty
Images; 6: Serban Enache/Dreamstime; 8: Ron Bull/Getty Images; 11: PhotoQuest/Getty Images;
12 background: scornejor/iStockphoto; 12 foreground: Seth Poppel Yearbook Library; 15: Tim Boyle/
Getty Images; 17: Warner Bros. Pictures/Album/Superstock, Inc.; 18: Spencer Platt/Getty Images;
20-21: The Estate of David Gahr/Getty Images; 22: David Corio/Getty Images; 24: catwalker/
Shutterstock, Inc.; 25: James Keyser/Getty Images; 26: Todd Plitt/Getty Images; 29: Spencer Platt/
Getty Images; 30: BillionPhotos.com/Fotolia; 31 top: DonnaSuddes/Thinkstock; 31 center top:
simonkr/iStockphoto; 31 center bottom: Ron Bull/Getty Images; 31 bottom: Scherl/Sueddeutsche
Zeitung Photo/The Image Works; 32: BillionPhotos.com/Fotolia.

Maps by Mapping Specialists.

TABLE OF CONTENTS

Meet Maurice Sendak

Children's books had always shown a world that was warm, safe, and cuddly. Then **illustrator** and writer Maurice Sendak came along. He wrote more realistic stories. He showed children standing up to fear and anger. He changed the world of children's books forever.

Maurice Sendak was born on June 10, 1928, in Brooklyn, New York. His parents were Jewish **immigrants** from Poland. He had an older sister and an older brother. Maurice adored his siblings. They were very close.

The Brooklyn Bridge is the most famous landmark in Maurice's hometown.

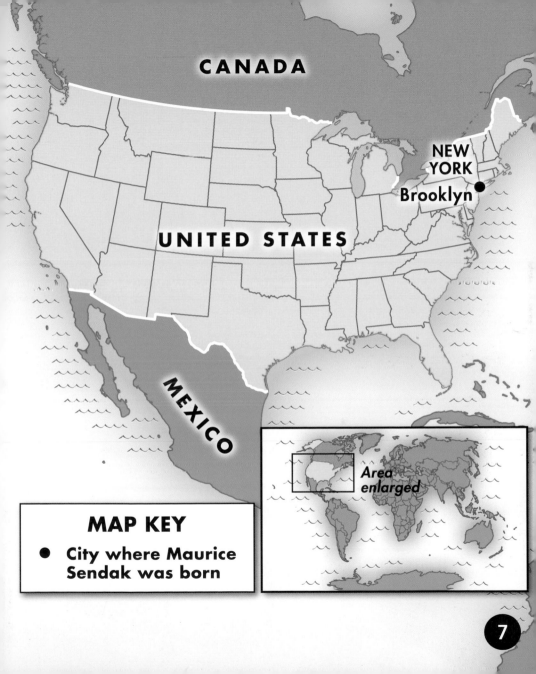

CANADA

NEW
YORK
Brooklyn ●

UNITED STATES

MEXICO

Area
enlarged

MAP KEY

● City where Maurice
Sendak was born

This photo shows Maurice with one of his drawings.

Maurice was often sick as a child. He learned to love drawing and reading. Both were quiet activities that he could do while resting in bed. He also liked watching the world outside. He noticed his neighbor Rosie playing outside his window. He thought she was bossy. But she had a great imagination!

FAST FACT!

Rosie later starred in Sendak's book *The Sign on Rosie's Door.*

In 1939, World War II began. Many countries around the world went to war. When Maurice was 13, the United States joined the fighting. Maurice was not old enough to be a soldier. But his brother, Jack, joined the U.S. Army. Maurice worried about Jack until he returned home safely at war's end.

People celebrate the end of World War II. The war showed Maurice that the world could be a scary place.

CLASS ARTIST
M. SENDAK

This is a photo from Maurice's yearbook. He was already an artist!

Becoming an Illustrator

Maurice and his brother used to make wooden toys together. They tried to sell some to a famous toy store called F.A.O. Schwarz. The store did not want to buy the toys. But Maurice got a job decorating the store windows. It was his first real job after high school.

The book buyer at F.A.O. Schwarz saw that Sendak was a talented artist. She introduced him to a children's book **editor**. The editor loved Sendak's drawings. She gave him his first children's book to illustrate.
It was called *The Wonderful Farm*. More projects followed. Soon Sendak started to write his own stories to illustrate.
He began winning awards.

This is the toy store in New York City where Sendak worked.

15

When Sendak was about 35, he wrote his most popular book yet: *Where the Wild Things Are*. It tells the story of Max, a little boy who behaves badly and is sent to his room. He then runs away to where the wild things live.

FAST FACT!

Sendak based the wild creatures in his book on his big, hairy (sometimes scary!) relatives. When he was little, they pinched his cheeks and said, "I could eat you up!" Sendak hated it!

In 2009, *Where the Wild Things Are* was made into a movie (shown here).

King of the Wild Things

Where the Wild Things Are won the Caldecott Medal. That is an award for the best illustrated book of the year. It bothered some people that the boy in the story was angry. But Sendak wanted to show a child dealing with strong emotions. That was a new idea. Kids loved it!

Sendak loved sharing his stories with kids.

Many of Sendak's books show a little white dog somewhere in their pages. That was his beloved dog Jenny. While she was alive, Jenny appeared in every book Sendak wrote. After Jenny died, Sendak made her the star of one of his books: *Higglety Pigglety Pop!*

Sendak loved dogs and owned many throughout his life.

Sendak was a big fan of Mickey Mouse. They even shared the same birthday!

When Sendak was little, he always wanted to stay up and watch bakers make bread at night. Years later, he wrote a book about it. It features a boy named Mickey and is called *In the Night Kitchen*. Some people tried to **censor** the book. They did not like that Mickey was shown naked. Sendak thought that was silly!

FAST FACT!

Mickey in the book was named for Mickey Mouse.

New Challenges

Sendak kept writing and illustrating. He also turned to other projects. He had always loved music. So he made *Where the Wild Things Are* into an opera. That is a play that is sung to music. Soon Sendak was working on other operas, too.

Sendak's Wild Thing was featured on a postage stamp.

Sendak poses with Max.

Sendak grew older.
He spent a lot of time on his Connecticut farm with his longtime partner, Eugene Glynn. He helped many illustrators who were just starting out. He also worked on new books.

Sendak poses with his dog Herman in 2005.

Sendak died in 2012, at age 83. But his stories and his wild characters live on. They continue to be treasured by children and adults all around the world!

Timeline of Maurice Sendak's Life

1928 > **1951** >

Born on
June 10

Illustrates first
children's book

Sendak's *Where the Wild Things Are* opera produced

1964 > **1980** > **2012**

Wins Caldecott Medal for *Where The Wild Things Are*

Dies on May 8

A Poem About Maurice Sendak

Kids can be angry, and kids can be scared.
Kids can be happy *or* sad, Sendak knew.
Kids can behave well, but sometimes they do not.
That's what he wrote about; that's what he drew.

You Can Be Creative

⭐ Write about or draw things you feel strongly about.

⭐ Do things your own way—don't be afraid to be different.

⭐ Let your imagination take you to wonderful places!

Glossary

- **censor** (SEN-sur): remove parts of a book, movie, song, or other work that are thought to be unacceptable or offensive

- **editor** (ED-ih-tur): someone who works with an author or illustrator to prepare a book to be published

- **illustrator** (IL-uh-stray-tur): someone who adds visual images to text

- **immigrants** (IM-ih-gruhnts): people who move from one country to another and settle there

Index

Facts for Now

Visit this Scholastic Web site for more information on Maurice Sendak and download the Teaching Guide for this series:

www.factsfornow.scholastic.com

Enter the keywords Maurice Sendak

About the Author

Jodie Shepherd, who also writes under her real name, Leslie Kimmelman, is an award-winning author of dozens of both fiction and nonfiction books for children. She is a children's book editor, too. She has never been to the land of the wild things, but she *has* been known, from time to time, to roar her terrible roar.